It's Time to Go...

Steve Mullins

Foreword by
Dr. Jonathan Oloyede

It's Time to Go...

Onwards and Upwards Publishers

Berkeley House,
11 Nightingale Crescent,
Leatherhead,
Surrey,
KT24 6PD.

www.onwardsandupwards.org

Endorsements

Steve Mullins has gathered together in one book a treasure chest of evangelism gems. The gem of simplicity, making it readable and understandable. Gems of challenge that every believer should expose themselves to. In this book, Steve has collected together a handbook, instruction manual, and a theological approach to the doctrine of the gospel with a call to passionate living and preaching.

Having served as an international evangelist for fifty-six years, I thoroughly recommend this book to men and women of all ages, denominations and nationalities. It will change your life and your approach to one of the most neglected subjects in the church today. This masterly presentation is undoubtedly part of God's strategy in raising an army of witnesses and evangelists in these closing days of time.

Dr Tony Stone
International Evangelist
Team Support Ministry

Steve's book is a great ministry resource for any Christian with a passion for evangelism. That should be all of us... It gives great practical insight into the heart and motivation for evangelism as well as many useful pointers in how to successfully share your faith. It delivers a powerful message that Christians need to grasp a hold of today if we as the body of Christ are to be effective in reaching more souls for the Kingdom of God.

Mark Oakes
UK Director
Christ for all Nations

Steve's passion fills the pages of 'It's Time to Go...' His book serves as a foundational reminder of the life-transforming message of the Gospel, and re-iterates the biblical challenge for each of us to share Christ and make disciples!

Andy Frost
Director
Share Jesus International & Crossing London

We need to express our gratitude to Steve for producing such an excellent evangelism handbook. It is written in a friendly, encouraging and easily accessible style that clears the obstacles many of us find hindering our personal witness. It is a good read and undeniably helpful. It deserves wide circulation. Those who read it are bound to become more effective ambassadors for the gospel, communicating with the same warmth and sensitivity that this book typifies. Thank you, Steve.

Hugh Osgood
President
Churches in Communities International

Contents

To Dad, gone but never forgotten –
thanks for inspiring me to follow Jesus.

"Trust in the Lord with all your heart, and lean
not on your own understanding; in all your
ways acknowledge Him, and He shall direct
your paths."

(Proverbs 3:5-6)

Foreword by Dr. Jonathan Oloyede

My heart was burning and aching as William spoke: "Jonathan, my mates are being knifed and killed by young men from Christian homes. They have turned away to other religions and vices due to the double standard and hypocritical lives of parents and church leaders. You seem different, Pastor, but can I trust that you are not fake?" This sanguineous young black man then looked me straight in the eye and said, "Are you for real, Jonathan, and do you really believe that revival can come to our streets and estates?"

I reached into my jacket to give him some money as tears and rain streamed down his face... and mine. Roberto was a Polish immigrant living on the streets of Tottenham. It was late at night and I had stepped out of my parked car off a main road in North London. A figure stepped out of the shadows and I stiffened instinctively. In these parts you could be mugged anywhere. This man was offering to sell me cheap stolen cologne. I turned towards him to politely decline when I was suddenly overwhelmed with so much compassion. I felt like weeping as I shared Jesus with Roberto right there in the rain.

I quickly realised that this avalanche of pure undiluted divine love coming from my heart was beyond natural. That night in the rain on the back streets of North London, I caught a glimpse of the depths of Jesus' love for souls. This compassion of God is real, tremendous, relentless and very emotional.

I remembered these two encounters as I read Steve's excellent piece about spreading the Good News of the Gospel of Jesus Christ to a needy world. As I look back over my own journey from Islam to Christianity, I am indebted to those who shared God's Love with me.

It seems there has been growing apathy and general malaise amongst church-attending Christians towards preaching or talking about faith in Jesus. In the West where I have lived for over two decades, the general attitude to outdoor, or one-on-one, sharing of the Gospel seems to be on the wane. There is a lack of confidence in evangelism and an apparent wimpy posture to boldly preaching the Cross.

We need to get back the estates, streets and leafy suburbs where unbelief, sinful vices and rebellion reign in human hearts. The only cure for this fallen world is the risen Saviour.

I shared my two encounters earlier to remind you and myself that the mission to reach and transform men's hearts is God's and not ours. He loves people more than us, and all we need to do is give Him the opportunity to draw people to Himself. God's Love will ooze through your words and actions as you share your faith in Christ.

You do *not* need to become a super evangelist or have many years of formal training to enable God to love anyone through you. All you need to do is eat, laugh, cry and relate with the others from your heart. The restaurant, the sidewalk, the library, office, kitchen, pub or car, your Skype, Facebook page or classroom are all sacred spaces for people to feel the warmth of Jesus' Love.

Let's begin the adventure!

Dr. Jonathan Oloyede
National Day of Prayer and Worship

Prologue

Evangelism: the Dirtiest Word in the World

Evangelism... The very mention of this word sends shivers down the spines of many Christians. Immediately the mind conjures up all kinds of stereotypical pictures of dodgy encounters with an outreach team, involvement with a cringe-filled evangelistic event or a seemingly overzealous evangelist. It seems that for most Christians, evangelism just isn't their thing. Therein lies a question from the start: is evangelism actually supposed to be someone's 'thing'?

Don't get me wrong, this book is not intended for the fainthearted. It will shoot from the hip. Actually, no! I hope it will shoot from the heart and that you will grasp something of my passion for evangelism. As someone once said, "Evangelism is something that is caught and not taught."

If you are looking for a deep theological treatise on evangelism, then this probably won't be the best book to read. If you are looking for all the answers to evangelism, then this book is not the book for you either. If you are looking for a down-to-earth, honest approach to evangelism that is Bible-based, then my hope is that this book will help you in a practical way. I trust that this book will stir your heart; that it will inform you, challenge you and motivate you to share the wonderful good news of Jesus Christ with those that God has placed in your path.

You may not be called to stand on a platform and speak to hundreds of people. You may not enter the realms of being a 'famous' evangelist and might not want to be (most Christians aren't called to that anyway), and if you do want fame from evangelism then you're harbouring the wrong motives to start with!

My prayer is that by the end of reading this short book your heart will be ignited to pray as the prophet Isaiah did – "Here am I! Send me." (Isaiah 6:8) – and that you will be obedient to the Holy Spirit's leading and embark on an adventurous life of evangelism!

CHAPTER ONE

It Must Be Love

I was there for all three. If I had the chance to live my life again, I'd still be there for all three; I wouldn't have missed them for the world. I don't know whether you are a parent or not, but being at the birth of your child is the most wonderful thing. Of course if you are Mum you don't have any choice about being there or not, whereas for Dad there are two options: to 'duck out' or to be present at the birth.

A long time ago, I heard a TV presenter introduce a well-known personality on his chat show. This celebrity was introduced as someone who was 'a born-again Christian'. At the time I thought it was a strange way to introduce someone. I'd been brought up in a Christian home and became a Christian when I was thirteen. I held the view that either you were a Christian or you weren't, which of course is true. What I had trouble working out was why the TV presenter placed so much emphasis in his statement on the fact that this celebrity was 'born again'.

I later came to realise the significance of this phrase (although I'm not sure this is the reason the TV presenter made the introduction the way he did!) Firstly, no one can be a *real* Christian unless they are born again (John 3:3)[1]; secondly, there is a kind of 'loose' view in society that if you attend church, pray, live a good life and maybe read the Bible occasionally, this will suffice.

You may have been somewhere and witnessed someone giving his or her life to Christ, and been a part of the 'event', but not actually

---

[1] This is covered in more detail in Chapter Two.

led someone to Christ; or you may have had the opportunity to lead someone to Jesus and know the joy that it brings.

However, when it comes to evangelism, the most attractive option for many Christians is to duck out. But is that how God intends it to be? In my experience, most people's 'problem with evangelism' stems from one of two misconceptions:

- "It is not my gifting."
- "I don't have all the answers and I might mess it up. What happens if I don't know what to say?"

Before addressing these, we need to lay a few foundations regarding the whys and wherefores of evangelism.

Called to relationship

I wonder if you remember the first date you went on, the first time you held hands with someone, the first time you kissed someone. How about the first time somebody told you about Jesus?

Evangelism starts with us. Well, actually it starts with God, but the job of *doing* evangelism lies with us. The Bible says that we were created to be in relationship with God. When God created the world, His intention was to be in relationship with the human beings He had created. That relationship was intact up to the point when Adam and Eve disobeyed Him. The moment they took the fruit from the tree that God had forbidden them to touch (see Genesis 3) their relationship with God was broken. Not only would they be separated from God and from being in relationship with Him, every other person born would suffer the same separation.

> **Romans 5:12**
> *Therefore, just as through one man sin entered the world, and death through sin, and thus death spread to all men, because all sinned...*

> **Isaiah 59:2**
> *But your iniquities have separated you from your God; and your sins have hidden His face from you, so that He will not hear.*

However, God in His love and mercy sent Jesus Christ to die for the sins of each and every person that has lived on planet Earth. The good news is that anyone who puts their trust in Christ as their Lord and Saviour can be forgiven of their sin and enter into the relationship with God for which they were intended. They will also be welcomed into heaven when they die.

More than just a ticket to heaven

Becoming a Christian is not just about getting a ticket to heaven though. We have a life to lead here, and God wants the lives we lead to be in relationship with Him. It's out of this relationship that our witnessing and evangelism should flow.

I don't know what you are passionate about (hopefully Jesus!) but I think it's fair to say that when a person is passionate about something, it won't take you long to find out about that passion. It will come up in conversation. They will have stories about it. It may be their pet rabbit, their photos, their football team or whatever, but they will want to talk about it. The things they are passionate about will soon become apparent.

Whatever a person is passionate about, you can rest assured it's not something that only takes up a small amount of their time and attention. They will spend time creating, organising and doing the things they are most passionate about.

God has made you, and He has created you to have a relationship with Him. That means He wants each one of us to spend time with Him. He wants us to get to know Him, to talk and pray with Him, to read His word (the Bible), and to allow Him to talk to us through it. He wants us to be filled with His Spirit. When we spend time with God it increases our love and our passion for Him.

It's out of this intimate relationship with God that our evangelism needs to flow, but often evangelism can seem like a burdening task that we have to participate in; except that we don't want to be burdened, so we don't do it. Evangelism is then viewed as being unimportant – an 'add-on' for churches. How many church meetings have you been to where the outreach programme is top of the agenda?

Of course, it's right for a church to consider and ask the question: what types of evangelistic programme shall we run? And of course it's true in the corporate sense that churches should run evangelistic programmes and outreaches. However, we are each called to be personal witnesses of Christ and to speak of what He has done for us in our own lives.

Whatever our connection with evangelism, be it personal or corporate (being involved with a church, or a group of churches in an evangelistic project), it has to flow out of our own personal walk with God. God loves each one of us. He made us to know Him and to love Him – and He wants us to let others know about this love too.

It's all about love

For us to be effective in our witnessing and evangelism, we must be filled with love: God's love. We must be lovers of God, and out of that we will be able to love the people that God has placed around us.

As Christians, we are to...

- love God
- love each other
- love those who have not yet come to faith in Christ

We cannot love our brothers and sisters in Christ unless we have experienced (and have a continual experience of) God's love at work in our own lives. We will look briefly at these three points in turn and use 1 John 4:19-5:5 as our baseline.

LOVE GOD

Someone once said, "To love someone is one thing, but to have them love you back is a totally different thing altogether." The Bible teaches:

> 1 John 4:19
> *We love Him because He first loved us.*

That is totally amazing; the God who created the whole universe, galaxies and stars loves each one of us!

It has been said that love is not a feeling but an act of the will, and to a certain extent that is true. If you have been in love with someone, you will know that when you first 'fell in love' it was quite emotional. But as time goes on, particularly for those in a marriage relationship, the way love is expressed can change.

Over time, the initial 'rushes of blood and fast heart beatings' no longer define love in the relationship; rather, love is a deeper understanding and growing appreciation and affection between two people. It becomes more of a daily choice: I choose to love you. So it is with God. He chose to love us, and as we grow in our personal relationship with God, our understanding of the love He has for us should deepen.

Not only did God choose to love us but He loved us when we were far from Him and not in relationship with Him. Do you know how hard it is to love someone and *not* to have them love you back? God showed us how much He loved us by doing just that.

Romans 5:8
But God demonstrates His own love toward us, in that while we were still sinners, Christ died for us.

God demonstrated His love by sending Jesus to die for us on the cross, so that the way would be open for us to be able to love Him.

So how do we love God? The answer is simple: by obedience. And obedience is expressed by loving one another.

LOVE EACH OTHER

1 John 4:20-21
If someone says, "I love God," and hates his brother, he is a liar; for he who does not love his brother whom he has seen, how can he love God whom he has not seen? And this commandment we have from Him: that he who loves God must love his brother also.

Our love for God is borne out in the way we treat our brothers and sisters in Christ. We may not realise it, but if people know we are Christians they will be watching us. They will see how we lead our lives, how we deal with certain situations, how we treat people, what we say and the way we say it. These are key areas in expressing and showing on a practical level the outworking of God's love in our lives.

"For us to be effective, we must be filled with love: God's love."

Jesus said to His disciples:

John 13:34-35
A new commandment I give to you, that you love one another; as I have loved you, that you also love one another. By this all will know that you are My disciples, if you have love for one another.

South American evangelist Luis Palau writes:

As you grow in the Lord, you begin to realise that people who love Jesus Christ are beautiful people. We may not see eye to eye with others on everything, but if we truly know and love Christ, we're all part of the same Body. What I'm talking about is quite different to phony ecumenism, which hides the truth: "You don't believe Jesus was born of the Virgin Mary? Oh, that's alright. We're one big happy family." There's a difference between that sort of ecumenism and the true unity of the Body of Christ of those who accept the basic truths of Christianity.[2]

However hard it may seem at times, it is possible to love our brothers and sisters "because the love of God has been poured out in our hearts by the Holy Spirit who was given to us" (Romans 5:5).

We need to recognise that loving others in the Body of Christ (the Church) on a human level is impossible because our lives are tainted with our own self-centeredness. However, the good news is that we can be empowered by the Holy Spirit, who enables us to live with the love of God in our hearts.

This is what is meant by a transformed life, and it is the central point of being a Christian. We are called to have a changed heart, and that is only possible through Christ. So not only are we to love our brothers and sisters in the Lord but we are also to love those who are not yet Christians.

LOVE THOSE WHO HAVE NOT YET COME TO FAITH IN CHRIST

Do you have a passion for souls? Do you long for the people you know to come to Christ?

Imagine if you knew someone who had a disease and was terminally ill. The only prospect ahead for this person would be death. You knew deep down that you had access to a medicine that

---

[2] Palau, L/Robnett TL: Telling the Story, p30 (Regal Books, 2006)

would cure them, but you didn't feel confident enough to tell them about it. Would this be a loving thing to do? I think you'll agree that it wouldn't. That's how it is with evangelism. The gospel is the answer to lives that have been devastated and traumatised by the power of the disease called 'sin', and God has called us as believers to be the ones to tell people that there is a prescription for this disease. All they have to do is take the medicine of the gospel.

Some may say that this illustration is too strong and that this type of example just causes people to feel guilty about not sharing their faith. I'm not saying we should be out there 'Bible-bashing' people; as we've already established, sharing our faith should be a natural evolvement that comes out of our own relationship with God. However, this does not negate the fact that sharing the gospel is an urgent matter. If we have no passion or desire to reach the lost, we need to ask God to give us that desire and passion.

God's love is powerful and strong. John 3:16 is often quoted as being the gospel in a nutshell:

John 3:16
For God so loved the world that He gave His only begotten Son, that whoever believes in Him should not perish but have everlasting life.

As believers, we have an instruction from God to go into the whole world "and preach the gospel" (Mark 16:15). We have been given the task of proclaiming the gospel to our families, friends, neighbours, work colleagues and whomever else God brings into our lives; to share God's love with them and to love them ourselves. As a note of caution, however, we need to ask ourselves the following question: do I love people because I want them to become Christians, or do I want them to become Christians because I love them? How far are we prepared to go to show God's love to people?

"Do you have a passion for souls?"

Jesus said:

John 15:13
Greater love has no one than this, than to lay down one's life for his friends.

Jesus made the ultimate sacrifice, and we need to be open to all that God asks us to do and be willing to do whatever it costs to share the gospel as we walk in obedience to Him.

Communication is key

When I got married, my wife and I had our wedding vows slightly altered. We recognised that for any relationship to be successful and to remain deep and meaningful there needed to be good communication, so in our vows we made a promise to each other to always communicate. That involves talking to one another, being open and honest about what we are feeling, even when it hurts. Over the years, communication has been a major key in our relationship.

Many relationships and marriages have broken up simply because a lack of communication was taking place between the couple that were involved in the relationship.

In the Christian life, prayer is imperative. Prayer is our way of communicating with God. It's how we talk to Him, share what is going on in our lives, tell Him how we are feeling, seek direction for our lives, and so on. Prayer is the doorway through which we can worship and praise God and thank Him for the things He has done in our lives. It is also the way that we can bring change to a situation.

We serve a living God, not one that is made of wood and stone. Our God hears us when we pray and He answers; He is a God in whom we can have complete confidence.

1 John 5:14-15
Now this is the confidence that we have in Him, that if we ask anything according to His will, He hears us. And if we know that He hears us, whatever we ask, we know that we have the petitions that we have asked of Him.

Prayer is so important in our evangelism. John Wesley is reported to have said:

Before we talk to the people about God, we need to talk to God about the people.

We need to be praying for the people we know. Who is on your prayer list? Who are you asking God to give you opportunity to speak to?

DL Moody said:

> *We ought to see the face of God every morning before we see the face of man. If you have so much business to attend to that you have no time to pray, depend on it that you have more business on hand than God ever intended.*[3]

There is nothing more important than praying that the people we know will encounter Jesus! We don't have to beat ourselves up over this; as we spend time with God we may find that He burdens us with someone in particular, and we get the sense that we should pray specifically for them. The important thing is that we pray, as we cannot expect God to move in people's lives if we don't.

So, in concluding this chapter, the cultivation of our own personal relationships with God is of paramount importance, not only for our own Christian lives but also if we are to be obedient to the call of God in taking the gospel to our next-door neighbours or to the ends of the earth. It flows out of our relationship with Him. Evangelism is not a task – it's a privilege!

Before moving on, take a moment to thank God for what He has done in your life. Ask Him to fill you afresh with His love, to enable you to share the gospel with those He sends your way. If you don't have a list of people for whom you are praying to come to Christ, take some time out right now to pray and allow God to bring to your mind people you know. Start to make a list and ask Him to open up opportunities for you to speak to them about Jesus.

---

[3] Palau, L/Robnett, TL: Telling the Story, p31-32 (Regal Books, 2006)

It's Time to Go...

Questions for reflection

What does it mean to be 'born again'?

_____

_____

_____

How do we express God's love through our own lives?

_____

_____

_____

Make a list of people to pray for.

_____

_____

_____

_____

_____

CHAPTER TWO

Clear as Mud

One of the main areas of resistance to evangelism I have come across over the years is the worry people have about sharing their faith in the right way and not messing things up. Maybe you've had a golden opportunity to share the gospel with someone but didn't take it because it went wrong once in the past. One thing to note here: God is much bigger than our mistakes. We just have to try to learn from them and move on. We will be dealing with some fears and objections to evangelism in the next chapter; however, I believe that most fears can be dealt with once we have a correct understanding of the gospel. If we are going to explain something to someone, then it is a great help if we have some idea what we are talking about!

This may seem strange to some of you reading this, and you may be thinking, "Why do we need to go over what the gospel is?" Well, you might be surprised at the number of people who claim to be Christians and yet don't have a clear understanding of the gospel and how to articulate it. I've been in many a meeting where an invitation to become a Christian was given (which is a good thing) and yet I was left feeling that the majority of what I believe should be included in the gospel had not even been mentioned.

This is a serious matter; we are dealing with where our friends, colleagues and fellow congregation members will spend eternity. We need to do everything possible to ensure that people understand what they are doing when they give their lives to Christ and how the decision will affect their lives. To make that happen we need to be clear on what it is we are sharing with them.

Of course, I'm not saying we need to cross every theological 't' and dot every theological 'i' when we share the gospel; however, I believe that scripture provides clear elements that need to be included. It may be that you will share all of these elements with someone in one conversation, or it may happen over a longer period of time. What is important, however, is that a clear, scriptural presentation of the gospel is given, and in a way that it can be understood by the listener. This may all seem a bit heavy, but just remember that the message we have is one of *good news;* that's what the word gospel means. It's this good news that we have the privilege of sharing with people.

In Chapter One we saw that evangelism should flow out of our own personal relationships with God. As Christians and believers in Jesus, we all have our own stories to tell of how we met Jesus and how He changed our lives; this can be a good starting point. However, if our aim is to lead someone to Christ, we need to make sure we don't leave key aspects of the gospel out, even when we are sharing our own stories. Having said that, there is no set formula for sharing the gospel, as in each conversation we need to be guided by the Holy Spirit.

Before we look at the key elements of the gospel message, it is important to be clear on what the gospel is *not.* For many, the idea of 'doing good works' and being involved in social action projects classifies as evangelism and proclaiming of the gospel. These things are all well and good. They are important. They are Christianity in action. They need to, and should be, taking place and playing a part in the life of an individual Christian and the local church. When we are involved in this type of work, we are making an impact because of the difference Jesus has made in our lives. But the question is, is it *evangelism;* is it proclamation of the good news?

What the gospel is not

IS THE GOSPEL ABOUT DOING GOOD WORKS?

Romans 1:16
For I am not ashamed of the gospel of Christ, for it is the power of God to salvation for everyone who believes, for the Jew first and also for the Greek.

When you wash your neighbour's car, is that "the power of God unto salvation"? How about when you buy shopping for a housebound neighbour or relative? Or when you visit a sick friend in hospital? Or when you give food to a homeless person? The list could go on, but the point is clear: as good as all these things are, they are not "the power of God unto salvation". Why not? Because the gospel changes lives; the gospel brings forgiveness and deals with doubt and unbelief. Salvation is about a person being made right with God and finding peace with God, having confidence that their sins are forgiven because of Jesus' death on the cross, and knowing that they have eternal life after they die.

As good as the acts of love listed above (and many others like them) are, they are not the gospel. They may be part of the process of someone coming to faith in Christ in that they are bridge-building activities, but in and of themselves they are not the gospel as the Bible talks about it. The Bible is very clear that the gospel is something that needs to be proclaimed.

John Peters argues:

> *Evangelism has to do with the proclamation of Jesus and Him crucified. No proclamation, no evangelism. I am not convinced that the 'spiritual warfare' we are called to as Christians has much to do with prayer. Though prayer which is focused on Jesus, his glory and his power to save, is essential to every effective evangelistic enterprise, we enter into direct conflict with the enemy by preaching the gospel, healing the sick, and casting out demons. No proclamation, no evangelism.[4]*

He continues:

> *I think that 'servant evangelism', in which we do surprisingly nice things for people like wash their cars when they haven't asked us to, is surely misnamed. Acts of service of this kind may lead to opportunities for explanation (though I suspect that the cynical English would often see through what is going on) but I still say no proclamation, no evangelism! We must be aware of every subtle and totally unconscious attempt to help us evade the challenge of preaching Christ and Him crucified. People liked*

Jesus when he healed and fed them; they were less keen when he made direct statements about his identity, purpose, and the implications for the way that life should be lived.[5]

IS THE GOSPEL ABOUT PASSING ON INFORMATION?

When we share the gospel, we are not just giving people information. We are giving them words that pertain to life.

In John 6, Jesus has to deal with a few of His disciples who were finding His teaching hard. Jesus had been speaking about the sacrificial death He was going to go through, and when He finished teaching some of His disciples said, "This is a hard saying; who can understand it?" Some of the disciples, although none of the twelve, even turned away (verse 66). Jesus responded to their questioning with words of comfort and power:

> **John 6:63 (emphasis mine)**
> *It is the Spirit who gives life; the flesh profits nothing. The words that I speak to you are spirit, and they are life.*

When we share the gospel we are sharing words of life:

> **Hebrews 4:12**
> *For the word of God is living and powerful, and sharper than any two-edged sword...*

I believe we need to become more intentional in our evangelism. Our aim is not to make friends (although hopefully we will); our aim is to win people to Christ. Evangelism has a purpose; it has an end goal, namely to see people commit their lives to Christ.

German evangelist Reinhard Bonnke writes:

> *The gospel is not history, though it is historical truth. The gospel happens. It becomes news when it is preached. You may call it anything you like – theology, the Word, the Truth – but if it is not articulated, it is not good news and the word gospel doesn't fit. Faith is not a truth that can be endorsed within the covers of a theological dissertation, put on the shelf and called the "gospel". The truth of the gospel can of course be written down,*

---

but the gospel is you and me telling the story of Christ, whatever the chosen means of transmission.[6]

Whenever and wherever we have opportunity to share the gospel, we are never just giving people information; we are giving them life-transforming words of life.

Defining the gospel

It's very useful to have what I call 'salvation verses' such as John 3:16, Romans 5:8, etc. memorised, as they can give us structure when sharing the gospel. And of course, as we have already noted above, the word of God is powerful and will do its own work. Many a time when standing on someone's doorstep the person at the door has not been interested in talking to me, but when I simply quoted a scripture verse it prompted a deeper conversation. That's not to say we should just start spurting out Bible verses to everyone we meet, but equally we must never underestimate the power of God's word.

1 Corinthians 15 also gives us a clear picture of the gospel:

> **1 Corinthians 15:1-4**
> *Moreover, brethren, I declare to you the gospel which I preached to you, which also you received and in which you stand, by which also you are saved, if you hold fast that word which I preached to you—unless you believed in vain. For I delivered to you first of all that which I also received: that Christ died for our sins according to the Scriptures, and that He was buried, and that He rose again the third day according to the Scriptures...*

The basics of the gospel are that God loved us so much that He sent His Son, Jesus Christ, to the earth to die on a cross for our sins; that Jesus was buried, rose from the dead, ascended to heaven and will return

> "We need to become more intentional in our evangelism."

---

[6] Bonnke, R: Time is Running Out, p72 (Regal Books, 1999)

one day. Jesus Christ, who knew no sin, became "sin for us, that we might become the righteousness of God in Him" (2 Corinthians 5:21). Although it's not a popular subject, we also need to make people aware that one day they will stand before God, on their own, to be judged. We need to emphasise that Jesus is the only way to heaven (see John 14:6) and that people need to come in repentance and faith to Him to receive forgiveness of their sin.

We talked earlier about being 'born again'. That is the aim of the gospel. A person who is separated from God because of his or her sin needs to be 'born again'. Jesus was very clear when He spoke to the religious leader Nicodemus. He explained:

> **John 3:3**
> ...unless one is born again, he cannot see the kingdom of God.

Many years ago, a pastor moved to a new church. The first week he preached on this verse. The second week he did the same, and the third, fourth and fifth weeks, until eventually someone came and asked him, "Why do you keep on preaching on the same verse each week?"

He replied, "Because you must be born again."

The pastor pressed the point home not only to emphasise the importance of the teaching but to make sure that everyone understood and acted on it.

Being born again is not about turning over a new leaf or pulling our socks up; it's something only God can do when a person comes to surrender his or her life to Him. Being born again is a supernatural act of God in an individual's life. When we are involved in evangelism, our part is to share the story of Jesus. It's the work of the Holy Spirit to bring conviction of sin and a release of new life to a person.

> **2 Corinthians 5:17**
> Therefore, if anyone is in Christ, he is a new creation; old things have passed away; behold, all things have become new.

I've found that it is useful to know a basic outline of the gospel, so I've put one together below. You could maybe use this or reword it, find other verses to add to it or put together one of your own.

THE PLAN

God loves you, God created you and God has a plan for your life.

John 3:16
For God so loved the world, that he gave his only begotten Son, that whosoever believeth in him should not perish, but have eternal life.

John 10:10
I have come that they may have life, and that they may have it more abundantly.

The problem is, most people don't have the peace and abundant life God wants us to have. This leaves us with a question: why not?

THE PROBLEM

God created us to be in relationship with Him. It's only through knowing and being in relationship with God that we can know and experience the abundant life God wants for us.

However, God didn't make us robots; He gave us free will and the ability to choose. The Bible says that all of us have chosen to disobey God and live our lives our own way. The result of this is that we are separated from Him because of our sin.

Isaiah 59:2
But your iniquities have separated you from your God...

Romans 3:23
...for all have sinned and fall short of the glory of God...

Romans 6:23
For the wages of sin is death, but the gift of God is eternal life in Christ Jesus our Lord.

THE PENALTY

If someone commits a crime and is caught, we would expect them to have to pay the penalty for this crime. We cannot pay the penalty for our sin against God because He is holy and sin cannot dwell in His presence. A price had to be paid for our sin, but we could not pay that price because we were separated from God by our sin. There is nothing we can do to earn our salvation – that's why Jesus came, died on a cross and rose again. Jesus paid the penalty for our sin so that we can come back to God and enter into a relationship with Him.

Ephesians 2:8-9
For by grace you have been saved through faith, and that not of yourselves; it is the gift of God, not of works, lest anyone should boast.

1 Timothy 2:5
For there is one God and one Mediator between God and men, the Man Christ Jesus...

1 Peter 3:18
For Christ also suffered once for sins, the just for the unjust, that He might bring us to God, being put to death in the flesh but made alive by the Spirit...

Romans 5:8
But God demonstrates His own love toward us, in that while we were still sinners, Christ died for us.

John 14:6
Jesus said to him, "I am the way, the truth, and the life. No one comes to the Father except through Me.

THE PROVISION

To receive forgiveness for our sins and to be able to enter into that abundant life, we must choose to follow Christ; to trust Him as our Lord and saviour.

John 1:12
But as many as received Him, to them He gave the right to become children of God, to those who believe in His name...

Romans 10:9
...if you confess with your mouth the Lord Jesus and believe in your heart that God has raised Him from the dead, you will be saved.

WE ARE NOT ALONE

One of the most releasing revelations I've had in terms of evangelism is that it's not all down to me! Yes, each one of us has a responsibility to share the gospel, and it is an urgent matter. If a friend we know is sick and we have the medicine, we had better make sure we give him the medicine quickly so he can recover. In the same vein, we need to be sharing the gospel. Millions are headed for a lost eternity and need to hear about Jesus.

We all have a part to play in reaching out to the lost, but although it is urgent, we cannot save anyone ourselves. Only Jesus saves. D M Cecil writes:

> Evangelism is not about you. Evangelism is about God and what He has done through Jesus Christ.[7]

In terms of salvation, God did His part in sending Jesus, Jesus did His part in dying on the cross, and now the Holy Spirit does His part by being the one to "convict the world of sin, and of righteousness, and of judgment" (John 16:8). We do our part in telling the story, but it is the Holy Spirit who does the internal work in a person's life and brings freedom.

We are not trying to win an argument when we share the gospel. If I just try to persuade someone that becoming a Christian is the right thing to do and that it will benefit his or her life, someone else will just come along tomorrow and persuade that person that their philosophy or ideology is better, and the person will be persuaded to change his or her mind.

As well as what the Holy Spirit is doing in the life of the person we are sharing the gospel with, we need to be sensitive to what the Holy Spirit is saying to us and the work He is doing in our own lives. There may be occasions where God leads you to talk to someone whose life He has already been working in and who is in a place to readily commit their life to Christ.

In Acts 8:26-39, we read the story of Philip and the Ethiopian eunuch. Philip has had great success in preaching the gospel in Samaria (Acts 8:4-8) and now God sends an angel to Philip and calls him to go south to the road between Jerusalem and Gaza. So Philip goes, and it just so happens that travelling on the road is an Ethiopian man. In fact, he isn't just any Ethiopian man; he is a man who has great authority under the Queen of the Ethiopians. It also just happens that this man is sitting in his chariot reading the Bible!

---

[7] Cecil, DM: The 7 Principles of an Evangelistic Life, p.13 (Moody Publishers, 2003)

The Holy Spirit leads Philip to run and overtake the chariot the man is travelling in. Philip overhears the man reading scripture and asks him if he understands what he is reading. There is a point to note when we are sharing the gospel: don't be afraid to ask the person you are talking to whether they understand what you are saying to them or what you have given them to read!

The Ethiopian then invites Philip to explain the scriptures to him, which Philip does. He uses Isaiah 53:7-8 as a basis for preaching Jesus to him. Another note here in our personal evangelism: start where people are at; look for links in so it is easier to share the gospel and use this opportunity to share Jesus.

As they travel, the Ethiopian asks to be baptised on the spot, and Philip obliges. Philip is then "taken away" and the Ethiopian goes on his way, rejoicing.

Some time ago, a similar incident happened to me. No, I wasn't carried away by the Spirit and transported somewhere else; neither did I meet a guy riding in a chariot! I was on a train...

On the particular week in question I had been with a friend of mine helping out with an evangelism training week. The team was being prepared to go and do some street work the following day (Friday), and one of the things we were asked to do at the end of the evening session was to pray for a 'divine appointment', to ask God to lead us to someone He had prepared for us to talk to. I was travelling home on the Friday as I had another commitment, but I prayed along with the others anyway and asked God for my divine appointment.

Friday came and I left the church and travelled home. Later that afternoon I was on the train to Victoria station, where I had arranged to meet my wife. As I sat in the compartment, just gazing out of the window watching the scenery go by, a young girl in her late teens or early twenties who was sitting across the aisle suddenly said, "Can I ask you a question?"

There was no one else in our part of the carriage, so I knew she was talking to me. I replied, "Yes!"

I assumed she was going to ask the time or how to get somewhere, but she looked at me and asked, "What do you do when someone you trust lets you down?"

Wow! That was not what I was expecting her to ask at all.

We began to talk and she started to share with me some of the troubles in her life, which were many and reasonably complicated. Our conversation continued until we had reached London, and we continued to talk as we got off of the train and walked towards the ticket barriers. I had been trying to answer her questions and give some advice, and then I just said to her, "Do you know why you asked me that question on the train?"

She looked a bit confused and replied, "No."

"Shall I tell you?" I offered. This made her look even more confused!

I explained that I believed God had led her to ask me the question and started to share the gospel with her. We walked through the ticket barrier in the main area at Victoria and just stood and talked for several minutes. She listened intently as I shared with her how much God loved her and how Jesus had died for her so that she might be forgiven and set free.

Eventually I asked her what was stopping her giving her life to Jesus right there and then. She paused and then replied, "Nothing."

So right there, at Victoria station, I led her to Jesus.

It wasn't until a while afterwards that I was struck with the thought, "That girl was the divine appointment that I prayed for yesterday!" After returning to London I had completely forgotten about my prayer the previous evening – but God hadn't.

We must always seek to be led by the Holy Spirit.

To sum up what we have discussed in this chapter, there is no better quote than this one by Douglas M. Cecil:

> *Evangelism is the communication of the good news of Jesus Christ – that he died for our sins and rose again – with the intent of inviting the listener to trust Christ. Evangelism is telling the Good News for the purpose of inviting the sinner to salvation.*[8]

What we have discussed here may all be 'old hat' to you, but I hope not! We should never get tired of the gospel. You may know the gospel well, but hopefully you have been challenged by some things in this chapter.

---

[8] Cecil, DM: The 7 Principles of an Evangelistic Life, p.36 (Moody Publishers, 2003)

It's Time to Go...

I'll close with one last challenge before we move on. When was the last time you shared the gospel with someone? The gospel is not just something we should gain knowledge about and keep to ourselves – it is for sharing! It may be good to just pause here for a moment and ask God to give you a clearer understanding of the gospel, and an opportunity to share it with someone soon!

Questions for reflection

Why is social action NOT evangelism?

_____

_____

_____

_____

_____

What steps can we take to help us communicate the gospel well?

_____

_____

_____

_____

_____

_____

_____

CHAPTER THREE

It's Not My Job!

"It's not my job!" If I had a pound for every time one of my children has said that to me when they've been asked to do something around the house, I'd have made quite a bit of money over the years!

Sadly, that's one of the main obstacles we face within the Church when it comes to evangelism: "It's not my job"; "I'm not gifted in that area"; "Oh, I think we should leave it to the professionals – maybe someone like Billy Graham"; "Speak to a stranger about Jesus? Oh, I couldn't do that. I wouldn't know what to say". These are just some of the excuses and objections that are raised when people are challenged to reach out to others with the gospel. Maybe you've used one of these or said something similar yourself. If you have, you'll be pleased to hear that you are not alone.

The Bible is full of people whom God called to do a job but whose initial response was "Not me, I can't do it, I'm not gifted" or "I'm too young, too old, or too unqualified". In a moment we're going to look at some of these people from scripture, but first I want you to take a moment or two to ponder this question:

What has God called you to do that you have not done because of who you are?

Or, to put it another way, what has God called you to do that you have not done because of who you perceive yourself to be? Quite often the person we perceive ourselves to be differs greatly from the person God says we are. When it comes to evangelism, we quite often lose ground before we've put a step forward; we've talked ourselves out of what God has called us to do because we believe something about ourselves that differs from what He has said about us.

Of course, there is a sense that left to ourselves we would be in trouble. We wouldn't be able to do what God has asked us and called us to do because, as Jesus said, "Without Me you can do nothing." (John 15:5). The amazing thing is that God has not left us to struggle on our own. He has promised not only to be with us (see Hebrews 13:5) but also to equip us for the tasks He calls us to – and that includes evangelism!

HIS WORKMANSHIP

We need to remember that "we are His workmanship, created in Christ Jesus for good works, which God prepared beforehand that we should walk in them" (Ephesians 2:10).

God has made us, created us, "in Christ Jesus". When we became Christians, our old lives were dealt with and our new lives began. An exchange took place – our old lives for new lives – lives that would be lived "in Christ". The joy for a Christian is that this new life brings new hopes, new dreams and new possibilities as we learn to trust Christ and allow Him to guide our lives, and that's the key!

In Christ, "all things are possible" (Matthew 19:26), and whatever we think, God will enable us and provide for us to do *all* that He has prepared and called us to do because we are in Christ. The Bible is full of people that the world saw as 'nobodies', but God took them and made them into 'somebodies'.

> 1 Corinthians 1:27-29
> *But God has chosen the foolish things of the world to put to shame the wise, and God has chosen the weak things of the world to put to shame the things which are mighty; and the base things of the world and the things which are despised God has chosen, and the things which are not, to bring to nothing the things that are, that no flesh should glory in His presence.*

A significant change

Now let's takes a look at some of the people in scripture who saw themselves as insignificant but whom God made significant. Consider Peter and John; they were simple fishermen, not theologians, not college professors, not company CEOs. They were just ordinary day-to-day fishermen that Jesus called to follow Him. They didn't always get it right; especially Peter, who ended up denying Jesus three times! It seems incredible that this is the same Peter who preached the first sermon on the day of Pentecost and saw three thousand people saved, but that's the mercy and grace of God. Peter was restored and became filled with the Holy Spirit, who enabled him to go out and boldly proclaim the gospel. He was a changed man!

Acts 4:13
Now when they saw the boldness of Peter and John, and perceived that they were uneducated and untrained men, they marveled. And they realized that they had been with Jesus.

You see, we are back to being in that relationship with God again. Spending time with Jesus changes us so that we can go out in the power, boldness and sensitivity of the Holy Spirit. Those who spend time with Jesus cannot help but become changed people as the Holy Spirit works in their lives to bring conviction of sin, which is then (hopefully) confessed. This leads to healing, forgiveness and restoration, and it brings us to a position from which we are able to respond to God in the right way. We then become equipped and empowered to go and do what He has called us and shown us to do.

When we enter into a relationship with someone, we don't get to know everything about them in one go. I've been married more than twenty years, and some days I feel like I am still getting to know my wife! Life is a journey, and as we journey with God and grow in our faith He will reveal more and more about Himself to us. Our part is to respond in faith and to trust Him every part of the way. As the apostle Paul writes:

1 Corinthians 13:12
For now we see in a mirror, dimly, but then face to face. Now I know in part, but then I shall know just as I also am known.

When we get 'saved' (give our lives to God), this is just the beginning of our relationship with God; we have started out on a journey of getting to know Him and finding out what He wants us to do. There are many times in life when heaven seems silent and when we feel unsure of the direction God wants us to take. However, there are certain things that are 'givens' in the Bible that are very clear in terms of what God wants us to do, and one of those things is telling others about Jesus!

Before we look at a few other characters in the Bible who struggled with their calling, let's just pause and ask a key question: what makes us feel insignificant?

Here are just a few thoughts. Maybe one of the following applies to you.

THE THINGS PEOPLE SAY ABOUT US

There is an old saying that I grew up with and that is still around today: "Sticks and stones may break my bones, but words will never hurt me." This statement is so untrue. What we say to and about people can shape their lives, possibly in a negative way. We need to be people that speak encouragement and blessing over people, building them up.

Proverbs 18:21 teaches that "death and life are in the power of the tongue". We need to be careful what we speak over someone's life. Maybe someone has spoken negative and hurtful things over your life. The first way of dealing with this is to forgive the person or people that have hurt you and spoken unkind words; the second is to receive the freedom that Jesus brings. We need to see ourselves as God sees us and not the way other people view us. Remember that we were created by Him; we are His workmanship. We would do well to also remember the words of David:

> **Psalm 139:14**
> *I will praise You, for I am fearfully and wonderfully made; marvelous are Your works, and that my soul knows very well.*

THE THINGS WE BELIEVE ABOUT OURSELVES:

As I just noted, what we say can shape a person's view about himself or herself. Our response to "You're stupid, you're worthless" will be so different from our response when someone tells us "You're brilliant" or "That's really good". If someone speaks negatively over us we will start to believe what they say. We will start to believe that we are no good, that we have no worth and that we will amount to nothing. This will result in a lack of confidence and brings us to a place where we feel that we will never achieve anything for God.

COMPARING OURSELVES TO OTHER PEOPLE:

I was once talking to a well-known evangelist about some ideas I had put together for an evangelistic project. I was talking about getting a number of other people involved to help spread the load. During the course of the conversation, he said something that has stuck with me: "God uses individuals." It was a real challenge to me, partly because of my own struggle with a lack of confidence in myself and partly because I had started to compare myself to others and what they were doing.

I learnt a valuable lesson from this. God has *made* us as individuals; there are things you can do that no one else can do in the same way. I am all for working with others and believe that this is extremely important. We have not been created as islands in the middle of the ocean and left to just get on with it with no one around us. We need each other and we need other people to help us as God leads. However, it can be easy to look at what others are doing and start to think that they are too far ahead, that we will never catch up. Let them do what God has called them to do! We each need to concentrate on what God has called *us* to do. Yes, some people will do things differently and sometimes possibly better than you, but just keep focusing on doing what God has called you to do. Remember that we were "created in Christ Jesus for good works, which God prepared beforehand that we should walk in them" (Ephesians 2:10).

I really can't do it!

Let's return to look at some of the people who had difficulty in moving forward with what God had called them to do.

> "Keep focusing on doing what God has called you to do."

MOSES

In Exodus 3 we read the story of Moses and how God called him to go and ask Pharaoh to release the Israelites from captivity in Egypt. Moses was out on the hillside tending the sheep when "the Angel of the Lord appeared to him in a flame of fire from the midst of a bush. So he looked, and behold, the bush was burning with fire, but the bush was not consumed." (Exodus 3:2)

Moses draws near to the bush to get a closer look and God speaks to him from it, requesting that he takes his shoes off as he is standing on holy ground. Moses obeys and God tells him He has heard the cry of the Israelites and has chosen Moses as the one to ask for the Israelites' release.

Moses is not ecstatic about this idea and starts a dialogue with God, citing the reasons why he thinks God has chosen the wrong guy for this particular task. Moses starts his argument by basically saying, "Who am I to go and speak to Pharaoh?" He is not at all convinced within himself that he is the right guy. He has been a fugitive on the run for forty years and at this point is just a humble shepherd. How on earth is the mighty Pharaoh going to listen to him?

Then, of course, there was a problem with the Israelite leaders themselves. How were they going to respond to this? What was Moses going to say when the elders asked him who had told him that he was the one to go to and deal with Pharaoh (Exodus 3:13)? Moses was full of questions and excuses, such as "Will they believe me; how will I convince them?" (Exodus 4:1) and "I'm not eloquent; I won't know what to say!" (Exodus 4:10). If these excuses sound familiar in relation to things you have said in the past when it comes to evangelism then don't worry – we'll deal with these in just a moment!

Before we look at the way God responds to Moses' objections, let's just look briefly at a couple of other well-known figures who argued with God about their callings.

GIDEON

The Israelites are again under oppression, this time under the Midianite army, and things are bad. The angel of the Lord appears to Gideon and tells him that the Lord is with him and that he is a mighty man of valour (Judges 6:12). Gideon's response to God is pretty much, "If that's the case and you are with us, then why is all of this happening?" and "Where are the miracles our fathers told us about?" The Lord then tells Gideon that he will be the one to save Israel from the hands of the Midianites! His response? "O my Lord, how can I save Israel? Indeed my clan is the weakest in Manasseh, and I am the least in my father's house." (Judges 6:15)

JEREMIAH

Jeremiah was called as a prophet to the nation of Israel. At the time of his calling, however, he was not convinced he was the right man for the job. He believed he was too young. In Jeremiah 1:6, we hear Jeremiah say, "Ah, Lord God! Behold, I cannot speak, for I am a youth."

It's very easy to look for excuses when it comes to sharing our faith, but I believe that if we can grasp just one thing it will transform our evangelism and our witnessing. What am I talking about? I'm talking about the same answer or promise that God gave Moses, Gideon, Jeremiah, Peter, John and each one of us, namely, "I am (or will be) with you!"

God has promised to be with us. Jesus said He would never leave us nor forsake us, and He won't. He is present with us through the Holy Spirit, who enables and empowers us to do what God calls us to do. We can have full confidence, as we pray for opportunities to speak to people, that God will be with us and that He will give us the words to say.

You have probably encountered many obstacles or excuses over the years when it came to sharing your faith, so we will briefly look at the three main ones now:

FEAR OF MAN – REJECTION

One of the issues we face when we are involved in evangelism is the fear that we will be rejected; that the person we are speaking to will take offence at what we say and reject us, especially if it is a close friend or family member. Of course, no one likes to be rejected, but there are a few things we need to bear in mind.

First and foremost, we are to fear the Lord. We are to put Him first, following his lead and direction for our lives.

Proverbs 29:25
The fear of man brings a snare, but whoever trusts in the Lord shall be safe.

God has promised to protect us and keep us safe. We need to pray that we will have the boldness to step out and speak when He gives us an opportunity. Of course, there may be many times when we 'bottle it' or even when we mess it up.

I had an incident like this just the other day when I was driving home from dropping my daughter off at school. As I drove home past a row of shops not far from where I live, two men were trying to get a big fridge-freezer into the back of a van. They were obviously struggling with it. As I drove past I felt a nudge inside me telling me to stop and offer to help. I didn't; I carried on driving.

I went over a small roundabout and a feeling of guilt started to rise up within me. "I couldn't stop," I reasoned. "There was nowhere to park." (I could have gone round the roundabout and pulled up onto the path with my hazard lights on; it would have been okay.) I carried on driving home, all the while regretting that I didn't stop and offer to help. "It's too late now anyway," I thought to myself as I pulled onto my driveway. But who knows what conversation I might have had with those two guys if I had stopped.

I suspect we've all have times when we feel the nudge of the Holy Spirit to do something and we ignore it. What we need to do is come before the Lord to ask for forgiveness and also for the confidence to speak up or share the next time an opportunity arises. That doesn't mean we can ignore what God asks us to do knowing that we can just ask for forgiveness afterwards, but we need to work towards being as consistent as we can in walking in obedience to His voice.

Secondly, if people do reject what we say when we share our faith with them, we need to remember that it is not us they are rejecting but Jesus Christ. Jesus Himself said:

John 15:18-19
If the world hates you, you know that it hated Me before it hated you. If you were of the world, the world would love its own. Yet because you are not of the world, but I chose you out of the world, therefore the world hates you.

Of course, we need to do our part in making sure that we act, speak and minister in a loving way, by making sure as much as we can that there is nothing about us that makes them want to reject us, such as not washing for a week or forgetting to clean our teeth for a couple of months! We must do all we can to make sure that we don't put people off, but we mustn't feel guilty if they reject the gospel when we have presented it to them in love.

FEAR OF GETTING IT WRONG – OUR OWN INABILITY

As we have seen, the Bible is full of people who struggled with their own inability. The key to dealing with this is that we come to a place where we recognise that we can do nothing without the help of the Holy Spirit.

We need to rely on the help of the Holy Spirit. He will bring to mind certain scripture verses and raise up gifts in us, such as a word of wisdom or knowledge that is specifically for or about the person to whom we are talking. Sometimes God uses us most when we are in that vulnerable place and we have to totally rely on His help. Again, we have to come back to the promises of Jesus:

> Matthew 10:19
> *But when they deliver you up, do not worry about how or what you should speak. For it will be given to you in that hour what you should speak...*

As we saw in Chapter Two, we need to have a clear understanding of the gospel, and we need to know and rely on the power of God's word.

All of these things (and you may think of others) help us in overcoming our worries about our own ability. As someone once said, "It's not our ability that God wants but our availability!"

FEAR OF RESPONSIBILITY – IT'S DOWN TO ME TO SAVE THE WORLD!

There probably aren't many people who struggle with this, but it does come up as an issue sometimes.

"We need to rely on the help of the Holy Spirit."

Let me be clear. Is it down to you to save the world? No!

Despite the urgency we should feel about the gospel and about sharing it with people, we are not to feel condemned with guilt if we haven't seen the whole of our town, city or nation saved because we personally haven't done enough. It's not all down to you. God has called each one of us into His body, and each one of us has a responsibility to share the gospel with those in our sphere of contact and influence. We have to find ways of connecting with those around us that provide us with opportunities to share Jesus with them.

Obedience is key

Many years ago I was on a tube train travelling across London. I was sitting quietly reading a book on prayer and spiritual warfare. Suddenly, out of nowhere, a voice inside me said, "Stand up and preach." I ignored this and carried on reading my book. A few moments later, it came again: "Get up and preach." Trying to deal with this, I began to concentrate on reading my book even harder but to no avail. I must have read the same paragraph about twenty times without really taking in what I was reading as God seemed to turn up the volume and repeated the call: "I want you to stand up and preach."

I sat there and started to feel physically hot. The carriage wasn't hot; I was just getting hot as my attempt to ignore this nudge to get up and preach continued. As I tried to concentrate even harder on my book, I glanced down the carriage and caught sight of a lady also reading a book. She was just turning it around as I looked up. I was sure that it was the same book I was reading, but I couldn't quite tell as she had turned it so that I could not see the cover.

Then I did something that I don't think I've ever done since, nor would I particularly advise anyone else to do. I had what I call a 'Gideon fleece' moment (if you don't know what I'm referring to, you can read about Gideon and the fleece in Judges 6:36-40). I said to God, "If she is reading the same book as me I will get up and preach." A couple of minutes (which felt like an eternity) passed before at last she turned her book around. It *was* the same book!

Straightaway I jumped to my feet and strode down the carriage towards her. "Are you a Christian?" I asked, leaning over the person sitting next to her. She looked up in surprise and nodded. "Great," I said. "Pray! I'm going to preach." I stood in the middle of the carriage and started to preach the gospel. Some teenage girls started to giggle, a businessman reading his paper lifted it higher so that his face could not be seen, while some stared into space and others listened to what I was saying.

What happened next was amazing. (No, the whole carriage didn't get down on their knees in repentance!) The train stopped in the middle of a tunnel for about two minutes. This meant that I didn't have to try to compete with the noise of a travelling carriage! As the train started to move again, I informed everybody that I would be getting out at the next station and would stand by the wall if anyone wanted to speak with me. Standing by the wall I watched and waited as people got off the train. Some gave me strange looks; others walked straight past. No one came and spoke to me.

I stood there until the train departed in case I had missed someone who wanted to speak to me, but there was no one. I must admit I felt a bit confused. Why did I need to preach if no one was going to respond?

Looking back on that incident I've come to two conclusions.

Firstly, maybe there was someone on that train who needed to hear what I had to say. Actually, I *know* there was, as everybody needs to hear the gospel. However, only eternity will tell as to whether that moment held any major significance for somebody in that carriage.

Secondly, it may have been a test of my obedience. One thing I've learnt over the years is that we may not always see the results we want to see or even expect to see from our ministry, but what is important is that we obey God and trust Him. Sometimes God may ask us to do things that seem totally strange and difficult. I had never preached on a tube train before and I've not done it since, but whatever God calls you and me to, our obedience to His voice, our stepping out in boldness, and our standing on and using His word are the keys to overcoming the obstacles and fears we face in our evangelistic efforts.

"It's not my job!" simply won't wash. We all have a responsibility to proclaim the gospel and we'll explore that in the next chapter; but before we move on, take a few moments to ask God to help you overcome your fears of sharing your faith and ask Him to enable you to walk in obedience.

May our prayer be that we heed the words of the apostle Peter:

1 Peter 3:15
But sanctify the Lord God in your hearts, and always be ready to give a defense to everyone who asks you a reason for the hope that is in you, with meekness and fear...

Questions for reflection

What excuses have you used to get out of doing evangelism?

_____

_____

_____

_____

_____

How can we overcome our fears?

_____

_____

_____

_____

_____

CHAPTER FOUR

Once Upon a Time

If you haven't picked it up yet, the common thread running through this book is that God wants to use people – ordinary people like you and me – to reach other people with the good news of the gospel. He wants us to reach them with the news that He loves them and that He cares for them, that without Him they are lost and will be lost for all eternity, if they don't have a right relationship with Him in the here and now. If we let God work through our lives, sharing our faith should be a natural overflow of our relationship with Him, and before we know it we're doing (yes, you've guessed it) evangelism.

But hold on a minute! This opens up a whole load of questions:

- Just because I get to share my faith with someone, does that make me an evangelist?
- Is everyone an evangelist?
- How do I know if I'm an evangelist?

Some while ago when I was on a mission in Uganda, I was walking through a village alongside the teenage son of my host and I asked him whether he knew what he wanted to do with his life. He replied, "I want to be an evangelist like you." He quickly followed this remark by asking the question, "What qualifies you to be an evangelist?"

I thought for a moment and then replied, "Well, I've been to Bible college, I have a piece of paper that says I've done a certain course and passed the grade; I have a lot of experience working in different situations, including Christian ones; but I don't think any of that

45

qualifies me to be an evangelist." I continued, "I think what qualifies a person to be an evangelist is what God puts in their hearts; it's the passion He gives us to tell others about Him."

Thinking about that now, it seems like quite a simplistic answer, but it's true nonetheless. So often we look to others to give us the affirmation, counsel and acceptance we need, which is right and good because "in the multitude of counselors there is safety" (Proverbs 11:14), but there is something deeper than this external counsel, something that God has placed within us.

As we have seen already, God calls ordinary people like you and me. That call is to follow Him and to tell others about Him. We may well go to Bible college or do some kind of training that may enhance the gift and calling that God has put on our lives, but I believe the thing that qualifies us is the passion and gifting God puts upon our lives and our obedience to follow the call He has placed within our hearts.

The context in which that young man asked me the question was a 'missional' context. I specifically went to Uganda to hold a gospel campaign, during which I would preach the gospel and see people respond to Jesus. However, this is just one of the many situations in which evangelists may find themselves working.

Indeed, there are many callings within the more general calling of the evangelist, and we'll take note of these in a moment. But first we need to answer the question that I know is burning inside you right now: what is an evangelist?

The Bible clearly speaks of those that are gifted and called as evangelists and of those that are witnesses. It is important to have a clear biblical understanding of what an 'evangelist' is and what a 'witness' is. There are differences, and we'll look at those differences here.

Am I an evangelist?

First of all, there is no such thing as a 'professional evangelist'. There are those that have been called and anointed by God to fulfil the specific role of being an evangelist and they have seen some wonderful fruit from their ministries, for example Billy Graham, Reinhard Bonnke, Luis Palau, Teresia Wairimu and a host of others. However, I'm sure each of these and the many others that have similar, maybe smaller, ministries would say that their ministries would be nothing without the work, guiding and help of the Holy Spirit. I've heard Reinhard Bonnke say that the Holy Spirit is the master evangelist. It is God who calls us and it is the Holy Spirit who equips us.

So, what is an evangelist, and what is an evangelist called to do?

The evangelist is primarily called to do two things: firstly to preach the gospel and lead people to Christ; and secondly to equip, train and motivate the Church to do evangelism. So if you have been sharing your faith, seeing people respond to Christ and encouraging other Christians to share their faith, then the chances are you have the gift of the evangelist.

One important point to note here though is that when people look at evangelists and their ministries, the following questions often arise: how successful are they; how well is their ministry going? That success gauge is often related to how many souls have been saved through their ministries. Of course, every true evangelist wants to see as many souls saved as possible, but seeing souls saved is not the only task of the evangelist. The second part of the work is just as important, if not more so – that of training others to become soul winners themselves. Multiplication is the name of the game!

Surprisingly, we only find the word 'evangelist' mentioned three times in scripture. The first reference is in Acts 21:8, where Philip is named as an evangelist. Others in the New Testament, such as Peter and Paul, were also evangelists, but there are no verses that specifically give them that title.

The second reference is found in Ephesians:

Ephesians 4:11-12
And He Himself gave some to be apostles, some prophets, some evangelists, and some pastors and

"God calls ordinary people."

> *teachers, for the equipping of the saints for the work of ministry,*
> *for the edifying of the body of Christ...*

This clearly shows that part of the evangelist's task is to help motivate, train, equip, mobilise and prepare each church to step outside of its four walls and share the gospel in the different spheres of society in which it finds itself.

The third scripture that mentions the term 'evangelist' can be found in 2 Timothy 4:5, where Paul writes to Timothy, instructing him to "do the work of the evangelist". It's interesting that Paul does not specifically call Timothy an evangelist but that he gives him the encouragement and direction to do the work of one.

Sometimes our first calling is not to be an evangelist – perhaps you are called as a pastor or a teacher – but whatever your call to leadership might be, I believe this admonition from Paul to do the work of an evangelist applies not only to all in Christian leadership but to the Church as a whole. Maybe some folk end up being pastors when actually they are called as evangelists. In some cases it may be that the person ends up being a pastor with an evangelistic edge; the important thing is that, whatever our role within the body of Christ, we should all aim "to do the work of an evangelist".

The word 'evangelist' means 'one who announces good tidings' or 'preacher of the gospel'. The stereotypical picture of an evangelist is the campaign evangelist or 'platform' evangelist, such as Billy Graham. Although some evangelists may have an itinerant ministry in which they preach from a platform to a large crowd, not all evangelists have this type of ministry. There are many other different types of evangelistic ministry that they are involved in, many of them operating within a very specific sphere of work.

There are church-based or community evangelists that work solely within the context of a local church and in the community in which the church is based. There are those that work with different evangelistic organisations or work as children's evangelists. Some have a calling to work with the elderly or out on the streets with the homeless. Some preach in the open air and some may use a sketch board. The list could go on.

Maybe as you're reading this you feel a tugging in your heart. Is God calling you to be an evangelist? If so, what type of evangelist would you be? What gifting has God given you?

Let's just consider some different ways of doing evangelism for a moment.

Personally, I'm very much a fan of what is commonly known as 'mass evangelism'. This type of evangelism usually involves many churches working together towards a gospel campaign which involves an evangelist preaching the gospel from a platform. There are maybe thousands of people in attendance at these events giving many the opportunity to hear and respond to the gospel. This preaching style is seen by some as very confrontational – it is however very biblical. The gospel is confrontational in and of itself. It confronts the sinfulness of humanity and it confronts the fact that, without Christ, each individual is headed for a lost eternity. The Bible asks the question, "How shall they hear without a preacher?" (Romans 10:14) and so whether it is in a stadium full of people, out on the street, or in a normal church service, the preaching of the gospel must take place!

Not everyone is called to preach though, and other ways of communicating the gospel are needed. Some people are gifted intellectually and are able to develop good, strong evangelistic reasoning to counteract those whose own intellect stops them coming to faith in Christ. People who have this type of evangelistic gifting may work in universities or write books on apologetics as international speaker and author Josh McDowell does. You may well be someone who enjoys a good intellectual argument and so find this strategy of evangelising easy. We must always remember though, we are not in this to win an argument, we are in this to win them to Christ, so our discussions should always be seasoned with love!

One area of life which we are all involved in is personal relationships with close friends and family. I've got to admit, sometimes sharing our faith with those closest to us can be the hardest thing to do. We need to constantly pray for inspiration and wisdom as

"What gifting has God given you?"

49

to how to share our faith with those closest to us as they are more likely, certainly at first, to be the ones who reject us. They see both the good and the bad from us; the key, though, is to not try to be something we're not but to walk in honesty and integrity as much as we can. They may try to argue against scripture but they cannot argue with our testimony – especially if we are living it out before their very eyes!

Personal evangelism doesn't just refer to reaching those close to us; it also includes reaching out to strangers by handing out tracts on the street, for example, or going door-to-door to talk with people. It's about reaching out to people one-by-one.

Many people are keen to talk about 'friendship evangelism', which is based on performing acts of kindness for people. Many assume that social action and doing good works are in fact evangelism. As we saw earlier, works of service and social action initiatives can act as bridges that enable conversations to start and lead into evangelism, but on their own they cannot be classed as biblical evangelism. Maybe you're great at showing people acts of kindness, but let me encourage you to look for opportunities to explain why you are doing these good works. As someone once said, "When you're doing friendship evangelism, don't forget the evangelism part!"

Maybe the things I've just mentioned still scare you to death; don't lose hope! You may not be a preacher or good at intellectual arguments, you may feel very uncomfortable sharing with your close family (hopefully by the time you finish this book you will feel more encouraged to step out in one of these areas), but there is something else you can do. Some may argue that this is not actually evangelism (and they may be right) but even though you do not feel confident enough to share your own faith, maybe you could have the confidence to say to somebody, "Why not come and hear so-and-so?" and invite them to a meeting or event at which the gospel will be preached or shared. Look out for meetings and events in your area that you think would be good to invite your friends and family to, where they will hear the gospel and have the opportunity to respond.

If no events are scheduled, talk to your church leaders and ask whether they will invite an evangelist to come and hold some meetings at your church. In John 4 we read the story of the woman at the well who, after meeting Jesus, went back to her city and invited people to meet Him: "Come, see a Man who told me all things that I ever did." (John 4:29) They came and many were saved (see John 4:39-41), all because of one woman's invitation!

There are probably other styles of evangelism you can think of or find in scripture, but one thing is certain: to be an evangelist you must have a burden for the lost; you must be looking for opportunities to speak to people, to pray for them and to preach the gospel.

Now I can hear those of you that know that you are not called to be out-and-out evangelists giving a huge sigh of relief: "Phew! I know I'm not called or gifted as an evangelist, so that lets me off the hook!"

Well, not quite...

The witness

As well as evangelists, the Bible also talks about a category that *every* Christian comes under: that of being a witness. A witness is someone who testifies about something he or she has seen and heard. This is where our current personal testimonies are helpful and needed, as well as our salvation testimonies.

The word 'witness' is used numerous times throughout scripture and can mean various things, including:

- Bearing testimony
- Being a martyr – one who bears witness by his or her death (e.g. Stephen in Acts 7)

Overall, being a witness is basically giving testimony (the facts) as to how God has worked, and is working, in your life. Jesus said to His disciples, "You shall be witnesses to me" (Acts 1:8). It doesn't matter how long you have been saved; if you have had an encounter with God – one that is hopefully ongoing – then you are to be a witness, to testify about what God has done and is doing in your life. It's something you live out; it's your lifestyle. God wants us to share our stories with others. It's not just about quoting scripture and Bible-bashing people; it's about telling *our* stories – that God is alive and well and is working in our lives!

When a trial is underway at court, say for a car accident or something, witnesses who saw the accident happen or were involved in the accident will be called to give their version of events in court.

What did they see? When did it happen? How did it happen? What difference did it make? How did it affect the people or property involved? Witness testimony is really valuable because the people giving evidence were there at the scene.

It's the same for each of us. If we belong to Jesus and our lives have been transformed by Him, we become His witnesses. We have our own stories to tell about how Jesus has changed our lives and what it means to us to know Him in a personal way.

What next?

Now that we have clarified the difference between an evangelist and witness, the next question is "If an opportunity to share comes up, what do I say?"

It's really useful to have a clear idea of your testimony. I know this may sound a bit ridiculous, as you know your own story only too well, but you need to be able to communicate that story in a way that can be understood by your friend, neighbour or the person with whom you are speaking on the street.

Here's an example of what not to say:

"Well, I was brought up in church, and then one day I was in a service and I realised I wasn't saved. The preacher was talking about being washed in the blood and I knew I hadn't been, and I thought to myself, 'I need to be washed in the blood!' So I ended up praying a prayer to God telling him I was ready to give my life to Him – and now I'm washed in the blood. Not only that; I've been justified, sanctified and redeemed! All because of the Lamb who died at Calvary, the Lamb who paid the price to set me free. Then after a while I was baptised. I told all my mates what happened and they have been washed in the blood too! We have a great time down at church, you ought to come sometime."

While all of the above may be true, people are unlikely to understand you if you share your story in this way. Terminology that may be understood by us as Christians may not be understood by those with whom we are looking to share our stories.

A good practical thing to do is to sit down and write out a brief summary of your testimony on a piece of paper. In the same way that we talked earlier about having a clear outline of the gospel, it's useful to have a clear outline of our testimonies that we can share in just two or three minutes. It's important that we give up-to-date testimonies. It's fine to talk about how you perhaps became a Christian twenty-five years ago, but we also need to include something about what God is doing in our lives today.

Sharing our testimonies can have a massive impact on people because they are personal. These things have happened to us and, as we noted earlier, no one can argue with our story. The word testimony means to 'bear witness' or 'to give evidence in support of a fact'. Your testimony is your evidence about what you have seen and heard; it's about the fact your life has been changed because of your relationship with God through Jesus Christ. It is not a fable, but a true statement about the way in which you now live your life.

In John 3:11, Jesus has a conversation with a religious ruler called Nicodemus and says to Him, "We speak what We know and testify what We have seen." (emphasis mine)

Your testimony is your personal experience of Jesus Christ and what He has done for you. A testimony must always point to Christ. Yes, it is your story, but it is your story of how Jesus changed your life. You may have amazing stories within your testimony, but the person must not just be left thinking, "What an amazing story!" Our stories must draw people towards Jesus.

It may be that your story is a little more 'colourful' than other people's. Maybe you are an ex-drug addict, murderer or thief and Jesus changed your life. Maybe your testimony is nothing like that. Maybe you were brought up in a Christian home and went to church and lived an 'OK' life before you actually made the decision to follow Christ.

Whichever is the case, we need to be careful not to give too much publicity to the devil! Even if our lives were really bad before we became Christians, we need

> "Your testimony is your personal experience of Jesus and what he has done for you."

to make sure that this comprises only a part of our overall stories. Your testimony should not be embellished or over-exaggerated to make it seem more exciting. Truth and integrity are key, and we need to make sure that we communicate that truth as effectively as we can.

It is quite likely that you will have the opportunity to share your testimony in different situations: maybe one-on-one with a friend or family member, or maybe in a church service or at a youth group. Each of these situations may call for a slightly different way of sharing, so it is good to have a variety of approaches up your sleeve.

It could be the case that time or other circumstances only allow you the opportunity to share one particular incident or aspect of your testimony. Possibly in a church service setting you will have less time to share than if you were sitting down over a meal and have the time to tell a longer version or the full version. In reality, though, the shorter and more precise you can get your testimony the better.

Structuring your testimony

So what should we include in our testimonies and how do we structure them?

The best place to start is the situation we were in before we met Christ. So you could say something like, "Before I became a Christian my life was going nowhere..." and then start to explain where you were at. What was going on in your life at the time? We need to give people a genuine, clear picture. We don't have to give them all the gory details, but we should tell them just enough to show that our lives were far from God before we came to realise our need of Him.

We then need to move on to what happened in the lead-up to our conversions and the point at which we came to understand the gospel. Maybe you were happily getting on with your life when a disaster struck, which made you start to ask questions about life. Maybe God spoke to you audibly when you were walking down the street one day. Perhaps you held long conversations with a friend that sparked a search in you to find the meaning and purpose of life. Or maybe you went to a meeting and heard someone preach the gospel message. Whatever your story, it's good to include the event or some of the events that started you on your journey to finding Christ.

Following on from that, the next part is key: how you actually came to give your life to Christ. For many of us, this will involve talking about the moment at which we realised or understood what the gospel means and prayed a prayer of salvation, either when we went forward at a meeting, prayed with a friend, or prayed alone in the quiet of our own homes. Some people are unable to define an exact date and time. The main point is to show that you are committed to Christ and that you are following Him.

Praying a prayer does not mean that we are saved. It's through trusting Christ and His work on the cross that we are saved. However, we are changed from the moment we receive Christ. It's important to communicate this.

Change is the next thing we need to cover in our testimonies. What changes took place in your life? Did you stop drinking, swearing or losing your temper? Did you have more joy? More peace? More love in your life? What change did Jesus bring to your life, and how did these changes affect you and those around you, such as family members, friends or work colleagues?

The final part of our testimony should focus on what God has done in our lives over the years (unless of course you have only just made a commitment to Jesus) and what He is doing in our lives today. How has God been faithful to you? You can talk about answered prayers or how God has been there through difficult times and helped you through. Mention something God is doing in your life today.

This may seem like quite a lot to fit into just a two or three-minute conversation, but if you take some time to think through and write out your testimony, it will help you to hone it and cut out bits that don't need to be included, such as deep theological words and jargon. Make sure you talk about Jesus rather than the denomination you belong to, and use some scripture verses to help back up your story, but remember that this is not a sermon, it's your story!

Sometimes I hear preachers suggesting that once you become a Christian everything in life becomes easy and everything in the garden becomes rosy. I don't know about you but that certainly wasn't my experience. God is there to help us through the storms of life as well as being there through the sunshine moments. Yes, we are victorious in Christ, but we are still in a spiritual battle and things do not automatically become easier once we decide to follow Christ. When we talk with others, we need to be realistic and avoid painting pictures that aren't quite true and that could cause people to stumble once they find out for themselves that things are not quite as we have told them. Again, integrity and truth are essential, and we have to continually ask ourselves whether what we are saying brings glory to God.

The aim of sharing our testimonies with people is that hopefully they will open doors for the gospel and become tools that the Holy Spirit can use in bringing the people we are sharing with to a place where they are willing to respond positively to Christ.

So as we end this chapter, the important news is that there are no get-out clauses. We are *all* witnesses, and some have been called to serve as evangelists too. We all have a responsibility to share our faith. Recognition of this responsibility shouldn't cause us to shrink back with guilt because we haven't been 'doing the job'. Rather, it should inspire us and release us to seek God in prayer and ask Him to enable us to become the best witnesses or evangelists we can be.

Before you move on to the next chapter, take a moment to reflect on what you have read in this chapter. Allow God to speak to your heart and ask Him to open up opportunities for you to share your story of how Jesus Christ has changed your life.

Maybe you've been struggling with your calling to evangelism and you're not sure which direction to take. Just take a moment to pray specifically that God would give you confirmation of what He is calling you to do, and ask Him to provide you with the means to do it.

Questions for reflection

What do you feel called to?

_____

_____

_____

How can you be sure?

_____

_____

_____

What steps will you take to start fulfilling your calling?

_____

_____

_____

_____

Chapter Five

Let's Party

Many years ago I was out shopping with my wife and two-year-old son. We went into a bookshop and after a few minutes she left me to go to the back of the store to buy a cup of tea, leaving me to browse for a few minutes. I finished my browsing and went to find my wife. When I found her I realised my son wasn't with her. She thought he had stayed with me and I thought he had gone with her. For the next few minutes we frantically ran through the store searching for our son and asking if anybody had seen him. Eventually I went out into the mall and there he was standing in the doorway of the store next door!

Relieved and happy, I picked him up and rejoined my wife, and we put our son straight back in the buggy. Our initial reaction upon realising he had wandered off was one of panic, worry and urgency, but on finding him we experienced great joy!

In Luke 15, Jesus told three parables about being lost: one about a lost sheep, one about a lost coin and one about a lost son. In each case when the sheep, coin or son was found there was a party. Jesus likened these stories to when a person becomes a Christian. In Luke 15:10, Jesus says, "There is joy in the presence of the angels of God over one sinner who repents." Isn't that fantastic? There's a party in heaven *every* time someone says 'yes' to Jesus!

I don't know if you have ever led somebody to Jesus and prayed with them to receive Christ, but if you have you will know that it brings great joy, both to the person who has received Christ and to the individual who has the privilege of leading them to Him.

Maybe you have not yet had the opportunity to lead someone to Jesus. Perhaps you didn't know what to say or how to handle the situation. Lots of people go part of the way and share their testimony and witness to somebody, but then they fail to 'close the deal' as it were and actually bring someone through to faith in Jesus Christ.

Of course, we can't force someone to make a decision for Christ and it's not just a case of getting someone to 'pray the prayer'. We're called to make disciples. Becoming a Christian isn't just about praying a prayer to make sure he or she gets into heaven while continuing to live life the same way. It's about that person putting their trust in Christ Jesus for their salvation and living in obedience and relationship with God through Him.

The main aim of every Christian's existence, apart from living a life of devotion and worship before the Lord, is to be a witness of Him to others. Although many of us find the task of 'witnessing' or 'evangelism' difficult, we are not alone...

Partners with God

In 1 Corinthians 3:9 we read that "we are God's fellow workers". That is an amazing statement. God has not left us alone to get on with the job. We work with Him and He works with us; we work together. That's why it is important for us to take time with God to pray and listen to what He is saying to us. We need to hear His voice and discern the direction He wants us to take.

The Bible is very clear that the salvation of people is very much on God's heart.

2 Peter 3:9
The Lord is not slack concerning His promise, as some count slackness, but is longsuffering toward us, not willing that any should perish but that all should come to repentance.

It is God's desire that people come to know Him and come into relationship with Him. When it comes to evangelism, or any other sphere of Christian life for that matter, we have not been left alone; God has given us the Holy Spirit to enable and equip us for the tasks that He calls us to do. There are plenty of really good books on the work of the Holy Spirit that discuss this in depth, but I just want to touch on a couple of main areas where we need to allow Him to work and guide us when it comes to evangelism.

First of all, we see in the New Testament that Jesus instructed His disciples to stay in Jerusalem.

Acts 1:4b-5
He commanded them ... to wait for the Promise of the Father, "which," He said, "you have heard from Me; for John truly baptized with water, but you shall be baptized with the Holy Spirit not many days from now."

He went on to say:

Acts 1:8
But you shall receive power when the Holy Spirit has come upon you; and you shall be witnesses to Me in Jerusalem, and in all Judea and Samaria, and to the end of the earth.

The disciples did not have any power, strength or courage in and of themselves. They needed the power of the Holy Spirit, and when the Holy Spirit came in Acts 2 we see that they were changed. They were empowered and they were equipped to do what God had called them to do: to go and preach the gospel. The wonderful thing is nothing has changed. The Holy Spirit is still at work enabling the work of evangelistic ministry to flourish and to be effective today.

Our evangelistic efforts won't amount to much without the Holy Spirit. Whatever kind of ministry we are in, we need His presence and power. In evangelism we find the Holy Spirit at work in two areas.

IN OUR OWN LIVES

The Holy Spirit is given to empower us to do what God has called us to do. We cannot work on our own; we must follow His leading. It is very clear in scripture that when the Holy Spirit comes He comes in power. He brings change. The Spirit empowers us to be bold and to speak out.

Sometimes at home our sink gets blocked. Over time, things go down the plughole that shouldn't and the pipe ends up getting blocked so that the water in the sink doesn't run away properly. Every now and again I have to put some sink-unblocking liquid down the plughole to keep the pipes clear and water flowing out as it should.

Our lives can sometimes be bit a bit like this, so we need to give them a check to see whether anything is blocking the flow of the Holy Spirit. We have to start with surrender and prayer, allowing the Holy Spirit to show us things in our lives that we need to deal with so that we can be effective in our ministry.

Being filled with the Spirit brings us to a place where we can be released into bold, effective evangelistic ministry as we learn to trust and rely on His leading. To fulfil our calling we need to continue in prayer, continue in the word and seek God to be filled with the Spirit.

IN THE LIVES OF THOSE TO WHOM WE ARE MINISTERING

What I am about to say now may come as a surprise, but it is true. You and I cannot convert anybody! Yes, you read that right. We cannot convert anybody!

Think about it this way. If we persuade someone to become a Christian, then someone could possibly come tomorrow and persuade them to become a Muslim, a Hindu or a teapot!

> John 16:7-11
> *Nevertheless I tell you the truth. It is to your advantage that I go away; for if I do not go away, the Helper will not come to you; but if I depart, I will send Him to you. And when He has come, He will convict the world of sin, and of righteousness, and of judgment: of sin, because they do not believe in Me; of righteousness, because I go to My Father and you see Me no more; of judgment, because the ruler of this world is judged.*

The Holy Spirit brings conviction of sin. It is the work of the Holy Spirit that brings a person to a place of repentance and confession, to a place where they can receive forgiveness and freedom.

Not everyone we speak to will be ready to commit

"We cannot work on our own; we must follow the Holy Spirit's leading."

to Jesus right there on the spot. Remember that we are aiming for, and praying for, our friends, work colleagues or family members to become 'born again'. Before natural birth takes place there is normally a nine-month pregnancy period as the child grows inside the womb. Often it is a similar situation when we are witnessing. I don't mean that it always takes nine months for someone to become a Christian, but the chances are that we will speak with that person over a period of time before they commit their lives to Jesus and become born again.

There are some statistics that suggest that it takes four years, on average, for someone to become a Christian. What is certain is that for most people their journey to faith takes some time. However, we must not let statistics control our thinking in evangelism. We need to remember that God can step into someone's life at any point. Just remember when Jesus knocked Saul off a donkey and his life was changed in an instant, and how in Acts 16 the Philippian jailer responded to Paul and Silas there and then after God supernaturally intervened with an earthquake.

Whomever we are ministering to – be it someone on the street we have just met or someone with whom we have had an ongoing conversation for many months – we need to discern where that person is in the commitment process. Does the person we are talking to have an awareness of God? If so, what do they understand about Him? Are they keen to find out more about Jesus and what it means to follow him? How open are they to what you have to say and, more importantly, to what the Bible says? Although the gospel is urgent, some people just won't respond positively, so we have to let it go. It may not be God's time, in which case we just have to leave them in God's hands.

As we share our faith and speak scripture into people's lives, the Holy Spirit takes what we say and uses it to speak directly to the individual's heart. Billy Graham wrote:

> *The Holy Spirit is the great communicator. Without His supernatural work, there would be no such thing as conversion. Satan pulls a veil over the truth, and this can be penetrated only by the power of the Holy Spirit. It is this third person of the*

Trinity who takes the message and communicates it to the hearts and minds of men and women.[9]

Prayer power

We need to bathe all of our evangelistic efforts in prayer. I don't mean 'efforts' in a sense that we are trying to do a good job, but it is vital that all of our conversations, our meetings, our speaking and our preaching that pertain to evangelism are covered in prayer.

We need to lay aside what we are and who we are and let Him take control. It is the Holy Spirit who gives us strength, power and anointing, and without the anointing of the Holy Spirit we will struggle to do what God has called us to do. We have to believe we can get the job done, but it is a job that we can't do on our own; we need each other and we need the help of the Holy Spirit.

The apostle Paul wrote these words:

Romans 15:17-19
Therefore I have reason to glory in Christ Jesus in the things which pertain to God. For I will not dare to speak of any of those things which Christ has not accomplished through me, in word and deed, to make the Gentiles obedient—in mighty signs and wonders, by the power of the Spirit of God, so that from Jerusalem and round about to Illyricum I have fully preached the gospel of Christ.

1 Corinthians 2:3-4
I was with you in weakness, in fear, and in much trembling. And my speech and my preaching were not with persuasive words of human wisdom, but in demonstration of the Spirit and of power...

Note, it was through the power of the Spirit that Paul was able to preach the gospel. He allowed the Holy Spirit to work through him, and we must do the same. You and I are to continue what Jesus started. We are to be His witnesses and to boldly proclaim the gospel. This is only possible through the power of the Holy Spirit working in our lives as we pray for people and seek to speak God's word into their lives.

---

[9] Taken from *A Biblical Standard for Evangelists*, by Billy Graham © 1984 Billy Graham Evangelistic Association. Used with permission. All rights reserved.

A few months ago we bought an old car so that my daughter could learn to drive. This car was a bit smaller than my car, but it was much more difficult to steer. At first it seemed strange that her smaller car was more difficult to steer than my slightly larger one. So what was the difference? My car has power steering and hers doesn't! The Holy Spirit has been given to us to bring empowerment to our lives: power to overcome sin, power to live right and power to help us share the gospel. The Holy Spirit is the power steering for our lives!

Leading your neighbour to Christ

So we have seen that our evangelism and witnessing must flow out of our relationship with God. We have also looked at what the gospel is and how to overcome fears and difficulties when it comes to evangelism. Now we come to the most important question of all: how do we lead someone to Jesus?

We are going to look at how we can help our neighbours, friends, relatives or work colleagues 'cross the line' and commit their lives to Christ. This can be the hardest part of evangelism, but it is the most rewarding and certainly the most important.

Imagine you have had several meetings and discussions with your neighbour about what it means to be a Christian and the difference Jesus has made in your life, but the big question of when they will give their life to Jesus continues to nag at you. "What else can I say? What more can I do?" People often become frustrated because the conversation has been going on for months but they have not been able to 'close the deal', and perhaps this is the situation you are facing.

Firstly, don't get too caught up in the trap of feeling stressed because a decision has not been made yet. You have been building a relationship with your friend or neighbour and that takes time. It is better to take the time and see a proper decision made than to rush things only for the seed that has been planted to wither away as quickly as it grew. Having said that, the gospel *is* an urgent matter, so we need balance.

It may sound obvious, but this needs to be said anyway: if you are seeking to lead someone to Christ, the whole process must be bathed in prayer. That is part of the responsibility God gives us in our evangelism. Prayer is key to our evangelistic efforts.

Here I will assume that you have been praying conscientiously for your friend or neighbour throughout the time you have been talking with them. In terms of them making a decision for Christ, the prayer has changed from "Lord give me an opportunity to talk to ---- about you" to "Lord, thank you for giving me the opportunities to talk to ---- for the past few months, but Father give me the boldness to now lead him/her to you and see him/her make a commitment to you."

There are two possible options in terms of you leading them to Christ. The first option would be the 'dream scenario': for your friend to ask, "So, how do I become a Christian?" The second option is a bit harder and would involve you taking the plunge at the appropriate moment and saying something like, "We've been chatting for a few months now. We've talked about various issues surrounding Christianity, and I've shared my story with you of what Jesus means to me. But what about you; what's stopping you becoming a Christian?" This is not a question to accuse them with but one that allows them to respond honestly. It can be asked in a gentle, sincere manner as you sit together in your sunny conservatory drinking a freshly made cappuccino!

One thing to note here is that there is a tendency for people to throw in 'red herrings' in a bid to move the conversation on to other issues or people. For example, they may ask, "What about people who have never heard the gospel?"

You can normally tell whether the question genuinely worries them or whether they are simply asking to throw you off track. Hopefully, as you have been getting to know them any key issues, concerns or problems they have will have been dealt with, so by now your friend should be ready to ask you (or ready for you to ask them) about giving their life to Jesus. The key thing for you to remember is to stay focused

"Prayer is key to our evangelistic efforts."

on the person you are talking to and not to become unnecessarily side-tracked.

So back to what happens next. The key question has been put and they have answered, "Nothing really!" – so there are no barriers in the way. Your friend has stated that he or she is ready to make a commitment to Christ. This is it – the moment you have been waiting for and praying for! So what happens next?

There are several things that you will need to make clear just to avoid any confusion. Of course, no one fully understands what they are doing when they first come to Christ. It is a step of faith. However, as they take this step it is useful to emphasise that they are not joining a church or a religion; your friend is surrendering his or her life to the living Lord Jesus Christ.

Before praying any kind of 'salvation prayer' together, it is useful to just briefly go over the gospel again. As I said earlier, it is good to have a number of 'salvation verses' memorised – or, even better, to have a Bible handy and get them to read out the verses for themselves.

As a reminder, here a just a few verses that I believe are key in leading someone to Christ:

- They need to understand that God loves them. (John 3:16)
- They need to recognise that they are separated from God by their sin. (Isaiah 59:2; Romans 3:23)
- They need to see that God has made a way for sin to be dealt with and for us to come into relationship with Him. (Romans 5:8)
- They need to see that God offers them an invitation and that it is an invitation to a new and eternal life. (John 1:12; 2 Corinthians 5:17)

There are obviously many other verses that can be used in this situation, so you can find others for yourself. However, it is good to just run over this brief outline with your friend. In summary, those who respond are doing five things:

- Recognising that they are sinners, separated from God by their sin, and that they have a spiritual need.
- Repenting (that is, turning away from all that they know to be wrong).

- Believing that Jesus Christ died for them on the cross.
- Receiving the Lord Jesus Christ through prayer, and by faith, into their lives.
- Starting a new life through the power of Christ working in them.

It is good, while going through these steps, to allow your friend to ask any questions or to make any comments. We need to talk in simple terms and use language they will understand by staying away from biblical jargon, but at the same time we must not dilute the truth of the gospel.

Also, although I have given an outline here, we must always be led by the Holy Spirit and listen to Him as we share the gospel and seek to bring people to Christ.

Once you have gone through these steps with your friend, you can then invite him or her to pray a prayer of salvation. This is an example of what you could pray:

> *Dear Lord Jesus Christ, I come to you now recognising that I am not perfect but a sinner. I confess my sin to you and thank you for dying for me.*
>
> *On the basis of your promises, I thank you that you are faithful and fair and will forgive my sin.*
>
> *I put my trust in you and ask you to come into my life by the power of your Spirit and make me new. Empower me to turn from all I know to be wrong.*
>
> *I receive your love, peace, and forgiveness, and thank you for the gift of eternal life that I now receive.*
>
> *Amen.*

It's as simple as that! Well, almost... as this is only the first step in this person's new journey with God. Your friend may say, "I don't feel any different," but you can assure them that this is normal; what they have done is taken a step of faith to trust and believe

"We must always be led by the Holy Spirit."

in a God who loves and cares for them.

Your job is not finished here, though. You now need to encourage your friend to read the Bible. Maybe you could buy them a Bible if you haven't already done so and suggest that they start reading through Luke's or Mark's gospel. They also need to learn to pray, tell someone else what they have done in becoming a Christian, and start to meet with other Christians. These are all things you can help with.

If you have never led someone to the Lord, start by making a shortlist of three or four people you feel God might be leading you to speak to, and start praying for them. Then look for opportunities to start speaking to them about Jesus.

Leading someone to Christ is exciting, especially if you get to know them quite well and can have further input when it comes to getting them started in their walk with God. May you know God's blessing and power as you seek to share your faith with the people God leads you to speak to and as you lead them into a relationship with the living Lord Jesus Christ.

Questions for reflection

What difference does it make to know that God partners with us?

_____

_____

_____

How can you allow the Holy Spirit to work more in your life?

_____

_____

_____

_____

What will you do apart from praying to reach out with the gospel?

_____

_____

_____

_____

_____

CHAPTER SIX

P.S. Now is the Time

If you are like me, there just doesn't seem to be enough time most days. There are so many things to accomplish in the fourteen hours or so that we're awake: work to do, shopping to take care of, places to visit, family to look after. The list is endless. Would it be any different if we had a thirty-six-hour day? Or a forty-hour day? Would life become less busy because we had more time? Somehow I think not. We would still find things to do with our time. We would still be too busy.

Although God is eternal and is not restricted by time as we are, He has not left us alone in this world to just get on with it. God has a purpose for this world. He has a purpose for you and a purpose for me. The psalmist wrote, "My times are in Your hand" (Psalm 31:15). It is a comfort for Christians to know that our time is in His hands; that our heavenly Father looks after us, protects us, provides for us and much, much more.

We need to dwell on that phrase "My times are in Your hand". As our time is in God's hands, that means God is in control. Our lives belong to Him, and therefore we should be conscious of how we use our time, what we do, what we say and where we go.

Ecclesiastes 3:1-11 provides a long list of how time is appropriated in life: a time to be born, to die, to heal, to break down, to build up, to weep, to laugh; the list goes on. The writer in Ecclesiastes concludes that "He has made everything beautiful in its time." Just think, God has made *everything* beautiful!

That seems so far from the world we see on our TV screens, though, or the world we read about in the papers or on the internet. The world we see is a world that is broken, hurting, at war, in turmoil and in distress; a world that looks far from beautiful. Could it be that the reason for this destruction in the world is due to the fact that so many people are living for 'now' in the world as they see it, without a God who cares? A world of self-centeredness and selfishness, where no real thought as to where they will spend eternity is given?

The heartbeat of anyone involved in evangelism is a heartbeat for the lost, a heartbeat of urgency. It is a heart that beats because God cares! The apostle Paul writes in 2 Corinthians 6:2, "Behold, now is the accepted time; behold, now is the day of salvation." The Greek word used in this verse for 'time' is 'kairos', meaning a 'season' rather than a defined length of time. God has not left this world to its own devices; He sent His Son, Jesus Christ, to die on a cross so that all who put their trust in Him could be forgiven and restored to a new life that has meaning and purpose.

This is the season we are in. This is God's now moment. This is *our* now moment. We only have the days we are alive to make a difference, in which we can go about "redeeming the time" (Ephesians 5:16). We only have now, this *season*, to share the gospel, to tell people about Jesus. So often we say that we are waiting for God, but the truth is He is waiting for us – waiting for us *to go*. For now is the time!

German evangelist Reinhard Bonnke once posed a question to his audience along these lines: "What you would do if you knew that you only had hours to live? Perhaps you would visit loved ones, get your finances in order and make some calls..." He answered the question himself by saying: "I can tell you what you would do. You would do the thing that was most important to you while you still had time!"

"The heartbeat of anyone involved in evangelism is for the lost, one of urgency."

71

In 1 John 2:18, we read, "Little children, it is the last hour." That means there isn't going to be another time. We are not here in preparation for another time. *This* is the time! This is our time and "it is the last hour". The seconds are ticking away, and the clock counting down to Jesus' return will soon strike midnight!

What are we to be doing in this "last hour"? What is important? Well, while we have health in our bodies and a calling on our lives, there is one really important thing we should be doing: making sure we are living out the life of grace God has enabled us to be partakers of as Christians. Now is the day of God's grace. We are never promised a tomorrow; we only have today; we only have now. Don't miss the opportunities God is sending your way. Don't leave it until it is too late.

As I write this, my son is about to take his school exams and I have been emphasising the importance of revision. The revision has to be done now; it will be too late to revise on the day of the exam. He has to make the most of his time now if he is to do well in his exams.

The same applies to our lives. We need to make the most of the opportunities God gives us now, while there is still time. Jesus said:

John 9:4
I must work the works of Him who sent Me while it is day; the night is coming when no one can work.

Someone once said, "Life is not a dress rehearsal." They were right; this is it! Just as Jesus had His 'now' time, so we only have the now to do what God has called us to do. One day I will not be here, I will have died. I don't know when that day will be, and you don't know when your day will come either. What we do know is that when that day comes for each of us it will be too late because "the night cometh, when no man can work".

This is not meant to be negative. For those who are in Christ, for those who have trusted Jesus and know Him as Saviour and Lord, the sting of death has been dealt with. Hallelujah! A day will come when we enter into eternity to be with the Lord Jesus forever. What a joy that will be! Until that day comes, however, we need to be alert, watchful and prayerful. And we need to share the love of God and the gospel wherever we can. We must work while it is still 'day', while we still have the opportunity and the time to do so. Friend, *it's time to go!*

Questions for reflection

Why is the gospel call urgent?

Dry Bones Trust

Dry Bones Trust is an evangelistic organisation founded and run by evangelist Steve Mullins.

As well as running African gospel campaigns, where hundreds have come to faith over the past few years, Steve has also travelled to several other countries to preach the gospel.

In the UK, Steve is leading an initiative called 'Now is the Time UK', which involves an evangelism training academy, evangelistic outreaches (fun days, community events, evangelistic preaching events) and the setting up of regional evangelists networks across the UK.

To find our more about Steve's ministry please visit:

www.drybonestrust.org

&

www.nowisthetimeuk.org

If this book has impacted you, challenged you, or helped you in anyway then we'd love to hear from you. Please email us at:

info@drybonestrust.org

Author's Recommendations

'Light, Love, Life' is a full colour 14-page booklet that gives a clear explanation of the gospel, and is an ideal booklet to give to family, friends, work colleagues, or for use during church outreaches.

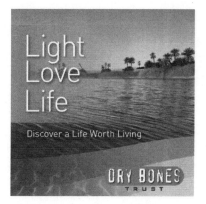

"As a pastor I have found the Light, Love, Life booklets incredibly useful in Christian Ministry. They have been very well received and I have found them to be a wonderful evangelistic resource." (Rev. M. Fitter)

'Happy Christmas?' is a full colour, 14-page evangelistic booklet that is ideal to give away at your carol service, toddler group Christmas party or other Christmas events.

Written by Steve Mullins, 'Happy Christmas?' gets to the heart of the reason for the season!

Find out more at: **www.drybonestrust.org**